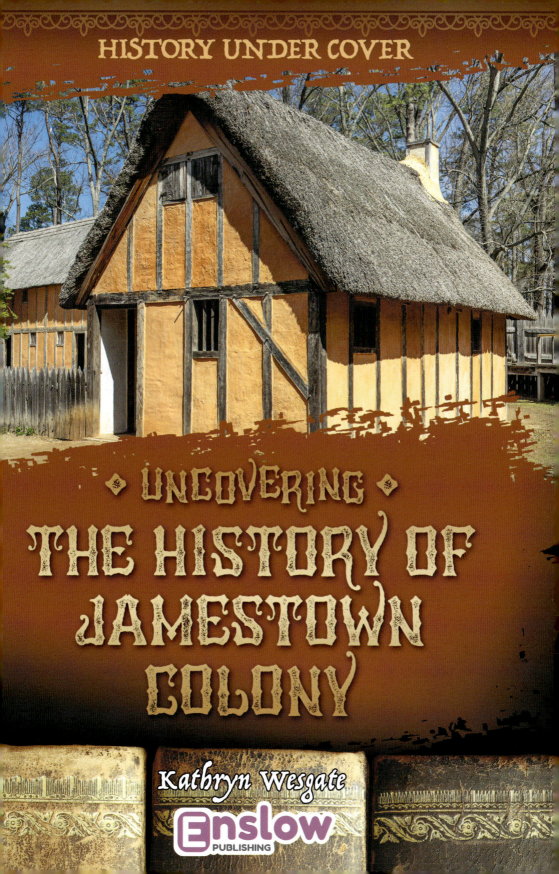

Please visit our website, www.enslow.com. For a free color catalog of all our high-quality books, call toll free 1-800-398-2504 or fax 1-877-980-4454.

Library of Congress Cataloging-in-Publication Data
Names: Wesgate, Kathryn, author.
Title: Uncovering the history of Jamestown Colony / Kathryn Wesgate.
Other titles: History under cover.
Description: New York : Enslow Publishing, [2023] | Series: History under cover | Includes bibliographical references and index.
Identifiers: LCCN 2021055296 | ISBN 9781978528871 (set) | ISBN 9781978528888 (library binding) | ISBN 9781978528864 (paperback) | ISBN 9781978528895 (ebook)
Subjects: LCSH: Jamestown (Va.)–History–17th century–Juvenile literature. | Virginia–History–Colonial period, ca. 1600-1775–Juvenile literature.
Classification: LCC F234.J3 W47 2023 | DDC 975.5/02–dc23/eng/20211123
LC record available at https://lccn.loc.gov/2021055296

Published in 2023 by
Enslow Publishing
29 East 21st Street
New York, NY 10010

Copyright © 2023 Enslow Publishing

Portions of this work were originally authored by Caitie McAneney and published as *Uncovering the Jamestown Colony*. All new material this edition authored by Kathryn Wesgate.

Designer: Leslie Taylor
Editor: Kate Mikoley

Photo credits: Photo credits: Cover, Claudine Van Massenhove/Shutterstock.com; series art (scrolls) Magenta10/Shutterstock.com, series art (back cover leather texture) levan828/Shutterstock.com; series art (front cover books) RMMPPhotography/Shutterstock.com; series art (title font) MagicPics/Shutterstock.com; series art (ripped inside pgs) kaczor58/Shutterstock.com; p. 4 Sidney E. King/https://www.usgs.gov/media/images/construction-james-fort-sidney-e-king; p. 5 From *The History of Our Country*, published 1899 ©UIG/Leemage/Bridgemanimages.com; p. 6 English School, (17th century)/English/Bridgemanimages.com; p. 7 https://commons.wikimedia.org/wiki/File:New_Towne,_Colonial_National_Historical_Park,_Jamestown,_Virginia_(14402603616).jpg; p. 7 (inset) https://commons.wikimedia.org/wiki/File:King_James_I_of_England_and_VI_of_Scotland_by_John_De_Critz_the_Elder.jpg; p. 8 https://commons.wikimedia.org/wiki/File:Jamestownsettlement.JPG; p. 8 (bottom) Claudine Van Massenhove/Shutterstock.com; p. 9 https://commons.wikimedia.org/wiki/File:Powhatan_john_smith_map.jpg; p. 10 https://commons.wikimedia.org/wiki/File:New_York_at_the_Jamestown_Exposition,_Norfolk,_Virginia,_April_26_to_December_1,_1907_(1909)_(14780176584).jpg; p. 11 William Ludlow Sheppard/Bridgemanimages.com; p. 11 (bottom) https://en.wikipedia.org/wiki/File:Jamestown_settler_dead_in_the_swamp.jpg; p. 12 https://commons.wikimedia.org/wiki/File:Captain_John_Smith_subduing_the_Chief.jpg; p. 13 English School, (17th century)/English/Bridgemanimages.com; p. 13 (map) Theodore de Bry/Bridgemanimages.com; p. 14 Tony Campbell/Shutterstock.com; p. 15 North Wind Picture Archives/Alamy.com; p. 16 https://commons.wikimedia.org/wiki/File:George_Percy.jpg; p. 17 https://commons.wikimedia.org/wiki/File:Jamestown_excavation.jpg; p. 18 North Wind Picture Archives/Alamy.com; p. 19 Everett Collection/Shutterstock.com; p. 20 North Wind Picture Archives/Alamy.com; p. 21 Colin Waters/Alamy.com; p. 22 Peter Frederick Rothermel/loc.gov; p. 23 https://commons.wikimedia.org/wiki/File:Howard_Pyle_-_The_Burning_of_Jamestown.jpg; p. 24 (bees) Rusana Krasteva/Shutterstock.com; p. 24 (livestock) BikerBarakuss/Shutterstock.com; p. 25 Joseph Sohm/Shutterstock.com; p. 26 https://commons.wikimedia.org/wiki/File:Pocahontas_1883.jpg; p. 27 (top) Science History Images/Alamy.com; p. 27 (wedding)https://commons.wikimedia.org/wiki/File:Marriage_of_Pocahontas.png; p. 28 https://commons.wikimedia.org/wiki/File:Jamestown,_Colonial_National_Historical_Park,_Virginia_LOC_2008627100.tif; p. 29 Timothy L Barnes/Shutterstock.com.

All rights reserved. No part of this book may be reproduced in any form without permission in writing from the publisher, except by a reviewer.

Printed in the United States of America

Some of the images in this book illustrate individuals who are models. The depictions do not imply actual situations or events.

CPSIA compliance information: Batch #CSENS23: For further information, contact Enslow Publishing, New York, New York, at 1-800-398-2504.

Find us on

Contents

Jamestown's Hidden History 4
Too Good to Be True 6
Occupied Land 8
A Rough Start 10
More Times of Trouble 12
A Time of Hunger 14
A Successful Crop 18
Growing and Changing 22
Changing History 24
The Real Pocahontas 26
A Piece of History 28
Glossary 30
For More Information 31
Index 32

Words in the glossary appear in bold or highlighted type the first time they are used in the text.

You may already know that Jamestown was the first permanent English settlement in North America. However, beyond the settlement's well-known history lies a darker past. Established in 1607, the settlement was far from successful in its beginning years. In fact, most colonists who came to Jamestown died shortly after arriving.

Early settlers work on construction at Jamestown, in 1607.

Located within the Virginia colony, Jamestown was started by the Virginia Company of London. The company hoped to make a profit in the New World. They expected to find riches, especially gold, and enough land for anyone who wanted it. Jamestown colonists hoped to settle the land, strike gold, and find a waterway to the Pacific Ocean for trade. Things didn't go quite as planned though. In fact, what actually happened nearly led to the failure of America as we know it today.

This artwork shows John White discovering the word "Croatoan" carved into a tree when he returned to Roanoke.

~ A Failed Settlement ~

Jamestown wasn't the first English settlement in North America, but it was the first permanent one. The title of first settlement goes to Roanoke, which the English established in 1585 on an island off the coast of modern North Carolina. That attempt failed, and colonists tried to settle there again in 1587. Soon after, their leader, John White, returned to England for supplies. By the time he came back in 1590, his people had disappeared, leaving behind only the word "Croatoan" carved into a tree. The disappearance of the Roanoke colonists continues to be a great mystery.

The Jamestown colonists wanted to start a settlement that would last. They made the long journey from England on three ships: *Discovery*, *Susan Constant*, and *Godspeed*. There were 104 men and boys on board the ships.

On May 13, 1607, the ships arrived at a location on the James River. There were no native peoples living there, and it was far enough away from the ocean to protect them from Spanish naval attacks. Deep water nearby meant ships could pull up close to the land to easily load and unload. In many ways, the location seemed ideal. However, it was far from perfect.

Native peoples chose not to live in the Jamestown area for a reason. It was marshy and wet. Although there was water nearby, it was often unhealthy to drink.

This piece of art shows what Jamestown may have looked like on the day it was founded.

King James I

Remains from an area where many Jamestown settlers lived, called New Towne, can be seen today at the Colonial Historical National Park in Virginia.

~ Proof of Jamestown ~

When they settled the land, the colonists named Jamestown after King James I. The settlement was a triangle-shaped fort. Each point had a strong wall for protection, called a bulwark. There were little houses and dwellings within the walls for the colonists. If the settlement wasn't successful and didn't last, how do we know what Jamestown looked like? In 1994, archaeologist William Kelso started excavating the site. His team found proof that Jamestown existed there, and over many years, they also found wells, graves, and building foundations.

The image many people see when they picture the place the Jamestown colonists landed is one of a rough, overgrown, unsettled area with as much land as the colonists wanted. This, however, is far from the truth.

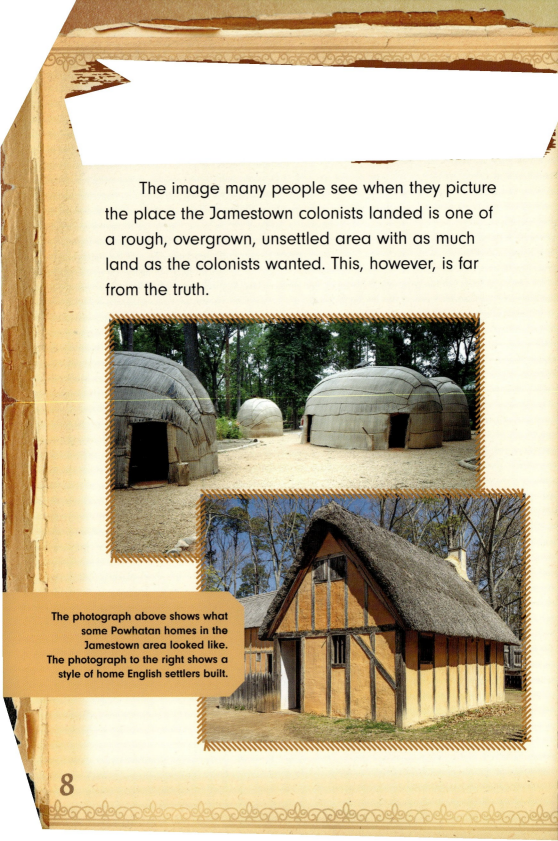

The photograph above shows what some Powhatan homes in the Jamestown area looked like. The photograph to the right shows a style of home English settlers built.

In reality, the colonists arrived to a land that was already well settled by native peoples. Though the exact site of Jamestown was unoccupied, about 14,000 Algonquian-speaking people lived in the nearby area. It was part of the huge empire of Tsenacomoco, which was broken into villages with hundreds of people each. The native people were experts on farming and living in this area. They burned trees to clear the forests and made huge cornfields. They had an advanced system of farming, which involved using land for a while and then leaving it to recover.

POWHATAN

~ Chief Powhatan ~

The leader of Tsenacomoco was Wahunsenacah, a strong and able chief. He's better known today as Chief Powhatan. When Powhatan was a young man, he gained power over an empire made up of six tribes. He **incorporated** many more tribes into the empire. It was a successful union, and he was the chief of all chiefs. When the English first arrived, Powhatan didn't lead any great attacks against them. In fact, in the beginning, Powhatan and his people traded with the English. They gave the colonists land in exchange for valuable guns, beads, and metal tools.

The English also called the people Powhatan led "Powhatans."

A Rough Start

The Jamestown Colony was originally led by a council of seven colonists. Early on, the colony faced hardship. Of the 104 men and boys who arrived in Jamestown, many died quickly. In fact, by January 1608, only 38 were left.

The colony needed a strong leader if it could ever survive. On September 10, 1608, John Smith became that leader when he became president of the colony. Smith was an English soldier and explorer. He wasted no time in exploring the area. He traveled to native villages to find food for his people. On one of his expeditions, Smith was captured and nearly killed. Once Smith was freed, he returned to Jamestown. A tough leader, one policy for his colonists was, "He that will not work will not eat."

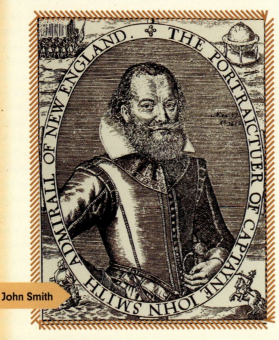
John Smith

10

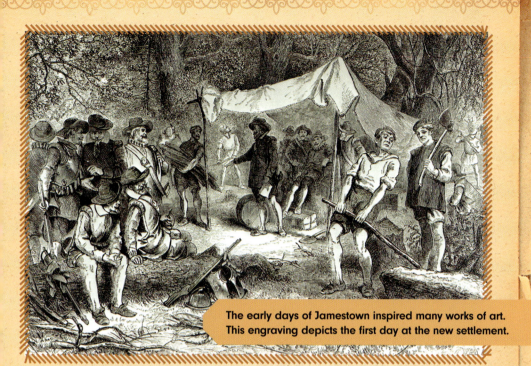

The early days of Jamestown inspired many works of art. This engraving depicts the first day at the new settlement.

This painting shows a Jamestown settler dead after going for water.

~ Causes of Death ~

Many history books report that early Jamestown colonists died of hunger. However, a historian named Carville Earle suggested it wasn't actually hunger that killed these people. Instead, he suggested, it was thirst. There's a theory that most died from diseases linked to drinking **contaminated** water. Some may have died from salt poisoning too. The river's water levels near Jamestown fell during the summer, and freshwater was replaced with salty water that wasn't safe for drinking. Still, some likely did die of hunger, as well as other illnesses.

More Times of Trouble

After a rough first year, things started looking up in Jamestown by the fall of 1608. Under John Smith's leadership, colonists were at work building, repairing, and planting. Two more shipments of colonists arrived as well.

Smith would do anything to keep the colony going. Unfortunately, that meant stealing from native villages, which greatly angered the Powhatan people. The relations between the colonists and the Powhatans became hostile, and attacks became more common. In this strange and new world, the colonists had no **allies**.

The colony became even more unstable when Smith had to leave suddenly. He was hurt in a gunpowder accident and traveled to England for medical help. Though he promised to send supplies, without Smith's leadership, the colony was about to face its most serious problems yet.

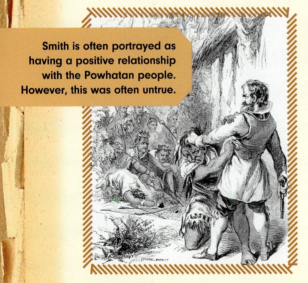

Smith is often portrayed as having a positive relationship with the Powhatan people. However, this was often untrue.

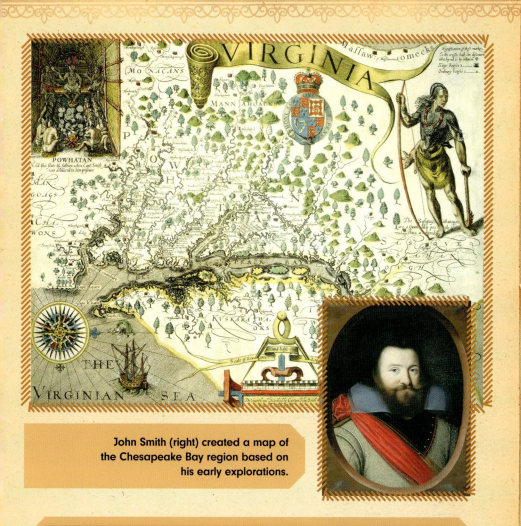

John Smith (right) created a map of the Chesapeake Bay region based on his early explorations.

~ The Real John Smith ~

When most people hear the name "John Smith," they think of the handsome, likable character from the Disney movie *Pocahontas*. The real John Smith wasn't so well-liked, however. In fact, he was put in chains on the journey to North America for plotting against other leaders. His leading style was one of tough discipline.

Smith became a soldier when he was only a teenager. He fought with the Dutch against the Spanish and with the Austrians against the Turks. As a soldier, Smith traveled from the Mediterranean to Russia and through Europe to northern Africa.

A Time of Hunger

If the colonists thought they were done facing hunger, the winter of 1609 to 1610 would prove them wrong. A great food shortage left two of every three colonists dead.

Leading up to that time, the area had experienced a 7-year **drought**. That meant there wasn't a lot of food available for anyone—natives or colonists. The colonists, unfamiliar with the land, hadn't been very successful in growing their own crops. They had once traded goods for food with the native peoples, but the hostility between them had grown.

Unsuccessful crops meant hard times for early colonists.

Chief Powhatan instructed his people to kill any colonist who left Jamestown. That meant people couldn't look for food outside of their small fort. Some colonists tried to leave the fort to find food, but if caught they were killed.

14

This image shows a group of colonists **rationing** their last few bits of food.

~ Another Disaster ~

In June 1609, nine ships of colonists left England for Jamestown. They had food and supplies to help the struggling colonists. However, a **hurricane** damaged the ships. Some finally arrived in August with a few remaining supplies. The main ship, however, was wrecked near Bermuda. After 9 months, survivors of that ship built two boats out of wood from the ruined ship and set out for Jamestown again.

The new colonists wanted Smith to step down as president. Smith didn't want to. His presidency still ended soon, however, when he had his gunpowder accident.

After Smith, a man named George Percy took over leadership of Jamestown. He left writings about the food shortage. These writings, plus unsettling details dug up by archaeologists, paint a troubling picture of the struggling settlement during a period often referred to as the "Starving Time."

When the colonists first ran out of food, they ate their horses. They ate dogs and cats, and even mice and snakes. When fresh meat ran out, some colonists ate the leather from their boots and shoes. Some used starch, normally for their clothing, to make a kind of porridge. Still, many colonists died from their hunger.

There were even reports of **cannibalism**. Often considered the darkest point in Jamestown's history, some people may have dug bodies out of graves to eat.

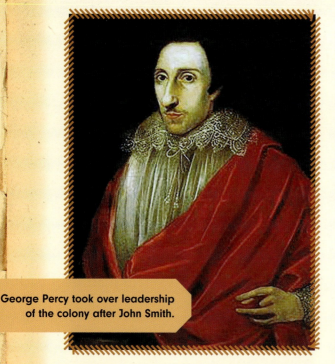

George Percy took over leadership of the colony after John Smith.

~ Proof in a Skull ~

About 500 colonists lived in Jamestown during the fall of 1609. By March 1610, fewer than 100 were still living there. Only some were lucky enough to have escaped by ship.

In 2013, archaeologists found proof cannibalism had occurred in the colony. They discovered a skull. Testing found that it belonged to a 14-year-old girl from England who likely died soon after arriving, possibly in August 1609. Her skull was cut in a way that suggested the attacker was trying to get to the brain, tongue, and other soft tissue—to eat!

Archaeological digs at Jamestown have revealed artifacts and skeletons of early colonists. Artifacts are objects made or used by people from the past.

A Successful Crop

When the shipwrecked colonists finally arrived in Jamestown on May 24, 1610, what they found was horrible. Few people survived the winter. Those who did were thin and ill. The group decided to leave. However, just as they were departing, more ships arrived with 150 new colonists and a good amount of supplies.

The Jamestown colonists finally found their first successful crop in tobacco.

John Rolfe was among the new colonists. He planted tobacco seeds that he'd found in the Caribbean. The result was a tobacco leaf that "smoked pleasant, sweete and strong," according to Ralph Hamor, secretary of Virginia. The crops were first sent to England in 1614. They were popular enough to compete in the mostly Spanish-controlled tobacco market. At the time, Spain controlled Central and South America and had declared death to anyone selling tobacco seeds to a non-Spaniard. It's unknown how John Rolfe got them.

This image shows John Rolfe tending to his crops.

~ Seeds of Success ~

Archaeologists at the Jamestown site made an important discovery in 2006. They found tobacco seeds that were hundreds of years old. They may be some of the seeds that John Rolfe used to plant tobacco in the New World. This was an amazing find since tobacco seeds are tiny. They were found in a well that had been used by the colonists. Pieces of tobacco pipes have also been found at the Jamestown site. Tobacco was the first successful cash crop in America.

This ship was used to transport tobacco from Jamestown.

By 1620, nearly 50,000 pounds (22,680 kg) of tobacco had been sent overseas from Jamestown. The colonists had finally found a successful crop. The settlement's population increased too. By 1624, at least 6,000 people had come to Virginia. The death rate was still high, but the colony was becoming well established.

Tobacco was good for the English, but other groups suffered for it. The English took land from the Powhatans. Unlike the native peoples, the English continued to plant on the same land each season. They planted mostly tobacco, while native peoples planted small amounts of many different crops. Tobacco takes a lot of **nutrients** out of soil, so it takes a while for the land to be usable for growing other crops again. Instead of finding a better way, the colonists took more land from native peoples.

As tobacco farms grew, white colonists made a profit. However, Native Americans lost their land, and many Africans lost their freedom. This image shows enslaved people landing at Jamestown.

~ Enslavement in Jamestown ~

In 1619, a ship called the *White Lion* brought enslaved Africans to Jamestown. The ship had captured around 20 Africans from a Portuguese slave ship. History books sometimes mark this as the beginning of slavery in North America. However, enslaved Africans were likely brought to the Americas in the 1400s, and enslaved Africans were likely in parts of what is now the United States as early as 1526.

Not much is on record about the enslaved people brought to Jamestown on the *White Lion*, but it is likely they played a large role in the colony's tobacco harvest.

Growing and Changing

While Jamestown was growing quickly, there were still few women in the colony. In 1620, a ship carrying nearly 100 women arrived at Jamestown so colonists could start more families.

The growing colony required good leadership. In 1619, the first representative legislative assembly in the British American colonies was formed. It was named the Virginia House of Burgesses after the name for the representatives: burgesses.

After a few years of peace, there was increasing **tension** between the colonists and native peoples. In 1622, a new chief named Opechancanough sent his men to attack Jamestown. Nearly one-third of the colonists were killed in the attack. Another deadly attack happened in 1644, but the chief was captured and shot.

In 1624, Virginia, along with Jamestown, officially became a royal colony. The Virginia Company came to an end.

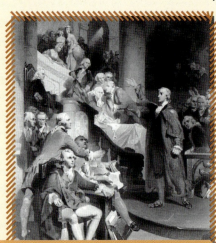

The Virginia House of Burgesses was made up of representatives elected by property owners.

~ Bacon's Rebellion ~

Burgess Nathaniel Bacon Jr. and other colonists were angry about the decreasing price of tobacco and laws that controlled its sale. They pinned much of their anger on native peoples, who sometimes attacked farms. In 1676, Bacon assembled a group of men to attack natives. Virginia governor Sir William Berkeley punished Bacon for his actions. Then, Bacon assembled a small army to march on Jamestown, which burned to the ground. The rebellion ended after Bacon's sudden death in October 1676. After the uprising, Jamestown was rebuilt. Another fire destroyed most of it in 1698, and it was finally abandoned.

It's clear that the arrival of the English at Jamestown changed the course of history for North America. The land—and the native peoples who lived on it—would never be the same.

Jamestown colonists introduced new animals and plants to the New World. This affected the natural ecosystems that existed there. They brought honeybees, which spread throughout the Americas. The bees **pollinated** several kinds of plants as they went, spreading plants that were native to one region to new regions. The colonists also brought livestock, such as pigs, cows, and horses. The native people didn't keep domesticated, or tame, animals. English livestock ate much of the native peoples' plants, walked on their crops, and ruined the soil. English colonists also cut down trees and native plants to create farms for themselves.

The colonists introduced honeybees and livestock to the New World. This affected the natural ecosystems that existed there.

This is a site where some Jamestown colonists were buried. Archaeologists have excavated, or dug up, much of it.

~ Bringing Illness ~

Some of the worst weapons of all that the English brought with them to the New World were diseases that hadn't yet spread to the Americas. Among the diseases was **malaria**, which is spread by mosquito bites. Malaria causes people to feel tired, have difficulty breathing, and develop a bad fever. Some people survive malaria, but get sick from it repeatedly. People who have no immunity sometimes die from it. Malaria has the power to weaken people, which may have made it harder for natives to combat colonists.

The Real Pocahontas

Much like John Smith, the truth about Pocahontas is far from the story of her character in the Disney movie named for her. To start, the name "Pocahontas" wasn't even her name. It was a nickname inspired by her playful character. Pocahontas's real name was Amonute, and she was sometimes called Matoaka. She was the daughter of Chief Powhatan. In the movie, she falls in love with John Smith. However, Pocahontas was only about 11 years old when the English landed.

When Pocahontas was around 14 years old, she married a man named Kocoum. Three years later, she was captured by the English and brought to Jamestown as **ransom**. She became a Christian, changed her name to Rebecca, and married John Rolfe. Pocahontas followed Rolfe to England in 1616 with their son. As they prepared to return to Virginia, she became ill and died.

Pocahontas

This work depicts how John Smith claimed Pocahontas saved his life when he was a captive of the Powhatans.

The work below shows Pocahontas's and John Rolfe's wedding day.

~ The Peacekeeper ~

As the chief's daughter, Pocahontas was often used as a peacekeeper. John Smith even wrote that she once saved his life. However, many experts think this never happened. What is true is that after John Smith was captured by the Powhatans and released, Pocahontas was sometimes sent to Jamestown with food for the hungry colonists. The young girl played in the fort with the other children. Later, because of Pocahontas's marriage to Rolfe, the English and Powhatans entered another period of peace. After her death, the relationship between the English and the Powhatans became hostile again.

A Piece of History

The events that happened at Jamestown forever shaped the history of America. During the Starving Time, it may have seemed that the settlement would fail, just as Roanoke had failed years before.

The early days at Jamestown were full of challenges. Archaeologists have uncovered many of the dark details of Jamestown's past, from invasive species to cannibalism. After more than 20 years of excavations, the archaeological team at Jamestown has reconstructed what the fort may have looked like, what kinds of tools people used, and even what they ate.

This image shows what a day in the life may have looked like when things were good for the colonists in Jamestown colony.

There are many mysteries surrounding the early days of Jamestown. In fact, archaeologists are still hard at work at the site, unearthing new discoveries all the time. While we may never know the full history of what happened at Jamestown, these discoveries will likely fill in some of the gaps.

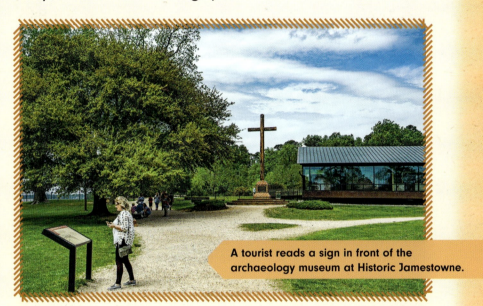

A tourist reads a sign in front of the archaeology museum at Historic Jamestowne.

~ A Visit to Jamestown ~

Jamestown Rediscovery is a project that began in 1994. It was launched by William Kelso, an archaeologist who first visited the area in 1963. At that time, it was assumed that the actual fort had been lost forever. It became Kelso's dream to find the fort by excavating the land. Today, you can visit Historic Jamestowne (how many colonists spelled it) and see the excavation site. Nearby, at the Nathalie P. & Alan M. Voorhees Archaearium, or archaeology museum, you can see thousands of artifacts.

GLOSSARY

ally: one of two or more people or groups who work together

cannibalism: the eating of the flesh of an animal by another animal of the same kind

contaminated: polluted

discipline: control that is gained by making sure rules are followed and punishing bad behavior

drought: a long period of very dry weather

hurricane: an extremely large, powerful, and destructive storm with very strong winds that occurs especially in the western part of the Atlantic Ocean

incorporate: to join together

malaria: a serious disease that causes chills and fever that is passed from one person to another by the bite of mosquitoes

nutrient: something a living thing needs to grow and stay alive

pollinate: to give a plant pollen from another plant of the same kind so that seeds will be produced

ransom: something that is paid in order to free someone who has been captured

ration: to control the amount of something that people are allowed to have

tension: a state in which people or groups disagree with each other

For More Information

Books

Freeburg, Jessica. *A Jamestown Colony Time Capsule: Artifacts of the Early American Colony*. North Mankato, MN: Capstone Press, 2021.

Rusick, Jessica. *Living in the Jamestown Colony: A This or That Debate*. North Mankato, MN: Capstone Press, 2021.

Uhl, Xina M and Philip Wolny. *Colonialism*. New York, NY: Rosen Central, 2020.

Websites

A Short History of Jamestown
nps.gov/jame/learn/historyculture/a-short-history-of-jamestown.htm
Find more facts about the English settlement here.

Jamestown from Home
historicjamestowne.org/education/jamestown-from-home/
Take a virtual tour of Historic Jamestowne by exploring maps, watching videos, and looking at artifacts.

Publisher's note to educators and parents: Our editors have carefully reviewed these websites to ensure that they are suitable for students. Many websites change frequently, however, and we cannot guarantee that a site's future contents will continue to meet our high standards of quality and educational value. Be advised that students should be closely supervised whenever they access the internet.

INDEX

Discovery 6

Earle, Carville 11

Godspeed 6

Hamor, Ralph 19

Kelso, William 7, 29

King James I 7

Opechancanough 22

Percy, George 16

Pocahontas 26, 27

Powhatan 8, 9, 12, 14, 21, 26, 27

Roanoke 5, 28

Rolfe, John 19, 26, 27

Smith, John 10, 12, 13, 15, 16, 26, 27

Susan Constant 6

tobacco 18, 19, 20, 21, 23

Tsenacomoco 9

Virginia Company of London 5, 22

Virginia House of Burgesses 22

Wahunsenacah 9

White, John 5

White Lion 21